Ancient Communities: Roman Life

ANCIENT ROMAN HOMES

Paul Harrison

press

New York

Published in 2014 by Wayland

Copyright © Wayland 2014

Wayland
338 Euston Road
London NW1 3BH

Wayland Australia
Level 17/207 Kent Street
Sydney NSW 2000

Series Editor: Julia Adams
Editor: Penny Worms
Series Consultant: Sally Pointer, archaeologist
Designer: Jane Hawkins
Picture Researcher: Kathy Lockley

British Library Cataloguing in Publication Data
 Harrison, Paul.
   Roman life.
   Homes.
   1. Dwellings--Rome--Juvenile literature. 2. Home economics--
   Rome--Juvenile literature. 3. Rome--Social life and customs-
   -Juvenile literature.
   I. Title
   640.9'37-dc22

ISBN 978 0 7502 8949 8

Picture ackoledgements:
Ancient Art & Architecture Collection: 25
Bardo Museum Tunis/Gianni Dagli Orti/The Art Archive: 23
Pat Behnke/Alamy: 18 Bridgeman Art Library/Getty Images: 7
British Museum /Werner Forman Archive: 27
Richard Broadwell/Alamy: Titlepage, 20
Orti Farnesiani, Rome, Italy/Bridgeman Art Library, London: 21
Werner Forman Archive: 13, 14, 29 Linda Kennedy/Alamy: 16
Araldo de Luca/Corbis: COVER (inset), 10, 19, 28
Museo della Civilta Romana, Rome/Gianni Dagli Orti/The Art Archive: 6
Museo Nazionale Archeologico, Tarquinia, Italy/Ancient Art & Architecture Collection Ltd/Bridgeman Art Library,
London: 4, 8 Museum of London: 5, 24R North Wind Picture Archives/Alamy: COVER (main), 9, 22
Paul Olding/Alamy: 26 Pompeii Italy/Alinari/Bridgeman Art Library, London: 12 The Print Collector/Alamy: 15
Jim Snyders/Alamy: 17 Sandro Vannini/Corbis: 24L WoodyStock/Alamy: 11

First published in 2009 by Wayland

Printed in China

Wayland is a division of Hachette Children's Books, an Hachette UK company.

www.hachette.co.uk

Contents

Words in **bold** can be found
in the glossary.

Empire builders

The Romans started as a tribe of people in Italy. Over time, their civilization grew and prospered. It became an empire that stretched west to Britain, east to the Caspian Sea, and down to northern Africa.

Built to last

The city of Rome was founded in 753 BCE and the Empire lasted until 476 CE. The Romans were excellent **engineers**. They built impressive public buildings, such as stadia for sporting events and shows, temples, grand houses, and apartment buildings. They also built **viaducts**, **aqueducts**, and a network of roads that stretched across the Empire. The quality of their work was often so high that some of the buildings they constructed are still standing today.

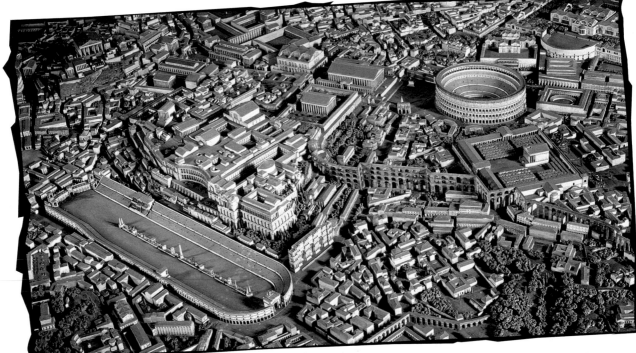

⬆ Up to one million people lived in the city of Rome. This is a model of the city center.

This relief shows a Roman blacksmith. He would have made everything from nails to armor.

Cost cutters

Constructing a large building requires a lot of expensive materials. Fortunately, the Romans knew how to make their buildings look impressive, while managing to cut costs. They discovered how to make and use a type of concrete, and it became a feature of their buildings. Often, the walls of their buildings were made of concrete and bricks, but were covered with a thin layer of **marble**. This made the walls look as if they were made completely from the more expensive marble.

A Roman object

Roman workers, builders, and craftsmen used tools that look almost exactly the same as the tools we use today. For example, the blacksmith in the picture above is using tongs and a hammer.

The first Romans

The first Roman homes were built on what is now called the Palatine Hill, near the River Tiber. It was such a good site that, over time, the entire city of Rome would be built on the Palatine and six other nearby hills.

Simple homes

The first Romans were often farmers and they lived in simple houses made of wood with **wattle-and-daub walls**. This type of house was easy to build but not long-lasting. As the Romans became more successful, these simple houses were replaced with more impressive and expensive stone buildings.

Romulus
[752–716 BCE]

The history of the early Roman rulers is a mixture of fact and fable. Romulus was said to have been raised by wolves along with his brother, Remus, but they grew up to become the founders of Rome. Most of this tale is a myth, but there was a Roman ruler named Romulus, who may have joined forces with a nearby tribe called the Sabines in the early days of Roman expansion.

⬆ Evidence of what early Roman homes looked like comes from Roman models such as this.

Etruscans

The Romans copied many of their building ideas from their powerful neighbors, the **Etruscans** and the ancient Greeks. Historians do not know very much about the Etruscans. Historians do know that they lived north of Rome and built large cities. For a while, the Romans even had Etruscan kings. Early Roman buildings were based on Etruscan ones, and it was from the Etruscans that the Romans learned how to build arches. However, the Romans improved on Etruscan building techniques. Roman arches could be made bigger and stronger, and they became an important part of Roman buildings.

Few Etruscan buildings have survived to this day, but their influence on the Romans can be seen in the pillars on sarcophaguses such as this.

Build it higher

By 2 BCE, Rome had become busy and crowded. It was difficult to find land for new housing. The Romans came up with a clever solution that we still use today—they built apartment buildings.

Room of my own

Roman apartments were called *insulae*. They were six or seven stories high, with a row of shops on the ground floor. *Insulae* were for poor city dwellers, and each apartment was little more than a single room with no kitchen or bathroom. Most Romans bought all their food from shops or bars instead, and they used public toilets and **bathhouses**.

People who lived in *insulae* often ate their meals in the shops below their flats.

Dangerous buildings

Since *insulae* were built for poor people, the builders often made them as cheaply as possible. This meant that they were badly built and would sometimes fall down without warning. To solve this problem, Roman leaders passed laws to stop *insulae* from being built too high. However, *insulae* were also renowned for burning down easily, because of the large amount of wood used to build them.

 Remains of *insulae* such as these can be seen at Herculaneum.

Nero
37 CE–68 CE

Nero was the fifth Roman emperor. He was disliked by the Romans because of his extreme behavior. He murdered his mother and his wife, and he had people executed for made-up crimes. However, he was also responsible for rebuilding Rome after fire destroyed the city in 64 CE. For the first time, Rome had an organized street plan, and the height of *insulae* was restricted to 57 feet (17.5 meters). Space was also left around buildings to stop any possible fires from spreading.

Homes for the rich

Not all Romans lived in *insulae*. Cities also had large, multiroomed homes called *domus*. A typical *domus* was not only a comfortable place to live, but it was also a **status symbol**, because only the wealthy could afford one.

⬆ This is an atrium of a *domus* in Pompeii. The atrium was the perfect way to add light to a home.

Light and airy

Romans wanted their homes to be as light and airy as possible. A *domus* was built around a central area called an **atrium**. The atrium had no roof, so it would let out the smoke from fires and let in light and rainwater. The water was collected in a pool to be used around the house for cleaning and washing. The rest of the rooms in the house were arranged around the atrium with a courtyard beyond.

Written at the time

Marcus Vitruvius Pollio was a famous Roman **architect**. In his book *De Architectura*, he described how rooms should be arranged in a *domus*:

"I shall now describe how the different sorts of buildings are placed as regards their aspects. Winter triclinia (dining rooms) and baths are to face the winter west, because the afternoon light is wanted in them; and not less so because the setting sun casts its rays upon them, and its heat warms the aspect toward the evening hours. Bedchambers and libraries should be toward the east, for their purposes require the morning light: in libraries, the books are in this aspect preserved from decay."

Religion

The Romans had many different gods, including the gods of the home, Janus and Vesta. Every *domus* also had a **shrine** in the atrium dedicated to spirits called *lares* and *penates*. These were the spirits of family members who had died and household gods who protected the family, food, and goods.

This shrine shows the household gods of a *domus* in Pompeii, Italy.

Living like kings

The Romans were proud of their origins as farmers and many dreamt of returning to this lifestyle. Many super-rich Romans did exactly that, but they did it in style by building enormous homes in the countryside, called villas.

Farming

Villas were really luxury farmhouses. They were surrounded by large areas of land called an estate, where dozens of slaves would look after farm animals and plant crops, such as wheat or grapes. Such farms were very important, because they supplied large cities such as Rome with much-needed food. Owners of villas had to be wary, though. Roman emperors occasionally took people's villas for themselves.

 These are the remains of the Emperor Hadrian's villa near Tivoli in Italy.

Publius Aelius Hadrianus
76 CE–138 CE

A fine example of a Roman villa belonged to one of Rome's most successful rulers, Publius Aelius Hadrianus, or Hadrian as he is known. Hadrian ruled the Roman Empire for 21 years until his death in 138 CE. He is probably most famous for building the Roman Wall—a *defensive* wall that stretched across England, from modern-day South Shields to Carlisle.

This is a bust of the emperor Hadrian. His villa is a famous tourist site to this day.

Fun house

Many villas were built outside of Rome so their owners could have a home in the city and one in the country. Over time, villas became more luxurious. Some villa owners stopped farming altogether and instead their villas became more like palaces. They used this type of villa to relax in style and show the world how rich they were.

Creature comforts

Roman cities were ahead of their time. Aqueducts brought fresh water into the cities and proper roads linked the whole Empire. Smaller Roman inventions could be found in the home, too, but only if the owners could afford them.

Warm and cosy

Roman homes were kept warm during the winter using the world's first type of central heating system, called a *hypocaust*. It was underfloor heating since hot air from a large **furnace** flowed through spaces between the ground and the floor. Hot air rises, so the *hypocaust* warmed both the floor and the room above it.

⇩ This is a view of the space under the floor of a Roman house with a *hypocaust* system.

Bathrooms

A *domus*, or villa, would often have its own bathroom. Unlike the ones today, Roman toilets could be used by more than one person at a time because they had lots of seats. The seats were built above running water, which carried the waste away into **sewage** pipes. This was a big improvement on the past, when people would have thrown their waste into the street.

A Roman object

Romans did not have toilet paper; instead they wiped their bottoms using sticks with sponges on the end. After use, these sponges would be washed in a small stream of water that flowed in front of the seats. The sticks would then be left for the next person to use.

 City apartments, such as *Insulae*, did not have their own toilets, so many Romans used public bathrooms.

Decoration and furniture

Roman homes did not have as much furniture in them as homes have today. Poor people often had nothing more than a bed. However, rich Romans liked to show off their wealth and taste by the way they decorated their homes.

Paintings and mosaics

Although Roman rooms did not have much furniture, the homes of the rich were highly decorated. Walls were painted and covered in bright frescoes (images painted directly onto the wall). Even the floors were decorated with pictures. These were called **mosaics** and were made of small, colored tiles that were cemented onto the floor. Mosaics were sometimes very detailed and cost a lot of money. Some can still be seen today in the remains of Roman villas.

This is a fresco in a villa in Pompeii. It shows a scene from Roman mythology of the god Dionysus marrying Ariadne.

Furniture

Romans enjoyed lying down. Apart from beds, couches were also popular items of furniture. Romans would half sit, half lie on a couch, even while eating, which could not have been good for their digestion. Beds and couches were made of wood and bronze. Cupboards were simple and made of wood. A *domus* or villa would also have had a wooden **strongbox** in which money, jewelry, and documents would have been kept.

A Roman object

Roman strongboxes were heavy, wooden containers that could be locked to keep their precious contents safe. Rather than being hidden away, the strongbox was often kept in the atrium of the house. To keep such a highly decorated and visible object more secure, they could be fastened to the floor with a metal rod.

⬆ Roman strongboxes were fitted with a padlock. This strongbox has a lock fitted to the side.

Gardens

The Romans borrowed the idea of gardens from the Greeks. Like all the ideas they adopted from others, the Romans developed the Greeks' idea of simple gardens to build luxurious parks of their own.

Luxury

The biggest and most dramatic private gardens were built around the luxury villas of Rome's super-rich. The gardens were **ornate** and were used to show off the owner's wealth and style. Water was an important feature of any Roman garden. The gardens would have had waterfalls and pools, surrounded by greenery, such as shrubs, bushes, and trees. These would have been cut into interesting and decorative shapes. Very few flowers were grown.

 Roman gardens were well-ordered and used water features.

⬆ These are the remains of the Emperor Domitian's impressive home, Domus Flavia.

Copycats

Romans in cities would copy what the important and wealthy people were doing, so gardens became popular in the cities, too. Even the smallest courtyard in a *domus* would have had plants growing there. Usually, these would be fruit trees or grape vines, because they were not only decorative, but they also provided food for the owner.

Written at the time

The Roman historian, Pliny the Younger, talked about his garden in a letter to a friend:

*"The drive is marked out with a box hedge, or rosemary where the box has gaps ... The inner part of the drive has a shady vine **pergola**, where the path is so soft and forgiving that you can walk on it barefoot. The garden is mainly planted with mulberries and figs, which this soil favors."*

The Roman household

Roman houses could get quite crowded. Apart from the family who owned or rented the house, there were often relatives living there, too. If the house was large, there would also be rooms where the house slaves would live.

Family roles

The head of any Roman household was the father of the family, or the oldest male member. The person who organized the running of the house was the wife and mother. It was her job to supervise the slaves and make sure there was enough food in the house.

 A Roman family welcomes a guest to their *domus*.

Slaves

All of the work in a Roman house was done by slaves, from cooking and cleaning to teaching the children. In fact, if it was not for slaves doing so many jobs, the Roman Empire would not have been as powerful or as large. Slaves were often people who had been captured in battle, or were the sons or daughters of slaves. Abandoned children would also be adopted as slaves. A slave's owner could grant the slave his or her freedom if the owner thought the slave had worked well.

This Roman mosaic shows a slave pouring wine for his master.

Written at the time

A Roman **philosopher** and writer, Seneca, warned fellow Romans to treat their slaves well:

"Remember that he whom you call a slave came into life by the same route as you, basks in the same sky, and breathes, lives, and dies in the same way as you do ... You look down at your peril at someone in whose place you could come to be, even while you look down on him ... This, however, is the sum of my advice: treat your inferiors as you would want to be treated by your masters."

Children

For Roman children, the home was more than just a place to live. It was where they learned valuable lessons about life, such as learning how to do a job or look after a household.

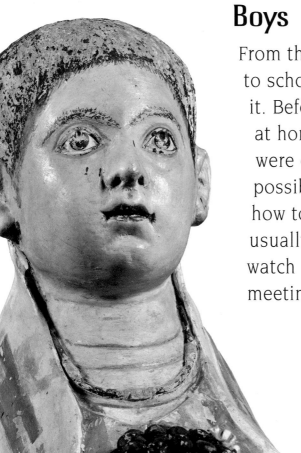

Boys

From the age of seven, boys were sent to school if their parents could afford it. Before then, rich children were taught at home by their parents. Poor children were expected to find work as soon as possible. Every male child would learn how to do his father's job. Romans usually worked from home, so sons would watch their fathers as they worked or had meetings to see how things were done.

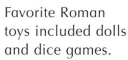 Favorite Roman toys included dolls and dice games.

A Roman object

Roman children would have learned how to write on wax tablets. These were pieces of wood that had been hollowed out and filled with wax. The child would then write on the wax with a piece of wood or bone called a stylus. When there was no room left, the wax could be warmed up and smoothed over, so the child could start again.

This is a wax tablet and stylus.

Girls

In Roman times, girls were not as respected as boys. In some poor households, they were seen as a burden and baby girls were sometimes abandoned. Even girls from wealthy families did not go to school. They spent their childhood in and around the home. They would learn from their mothers how to sew and run a household. This was to prepare them for married life, which, for Roman girls, could begin as young as 12 years old.

Homes abroad

When the Romans conquered new countries, they brought their ideas on how to do things with them. They changed the way the countries were run, the type of money that was used, and even the way their homes were built.

Northern Europe

When Britain and northern Europe were made part of the Empire, the Roman house must have come as a surprise. The usual British house was made of wood and **daub** with a thatched roof, and was generally round in shape. Roman villas, on the other hand, were made of brick and stone. Although most Britons continued to live in roundhouses, British tribal chiefs who accepted Roman rule moved into grand villas. There they discovered the benefits of other Roman inventions, such as central heating.

There is little evidence left of what British roundhouses looked like, but it is believed that they were similar to this reconstruction.

Egypt

Traditional Egyptian houses were made from mud bricks and were either one or two stories high. Some historians claim that after Egypt became part of the Roman Empire, a new kind of house was introduced. For example, the ruins of a town called Karanis show multistory apartment buildings that look like Roman *insulae*.

This is a model of an Egyptian town house. It is three stories high and has a flat roof.

Written at the time

During the Roman period, Egyptian homeowners could own a complete house, or just part of a house. This could get quite confusing, as this **census** from Karanis in 189 CE shows:

"..to Gaia Apolinaria and Gemellus Horion…a house and two courtyards, formerly the property of Valeria Diodora, and a third share of two houses and two courtyards, and elsewhere a half share of a house and courtyard, and of another courtyard, and elsewhere a house and courtyard, and two courtyards, formerly the property of Gains Longinus Apolinarius…and elsewhere a third share of a house and courtyard."

Timeline

BCE

753	Start of the Roman Empire
509	Kings expelled—start of the Roman Republic
450	Romans draw up their first set of laws known as the Twelve Tables
378	Wall built around the city of Rome
272	Rome takes control of all of Italy
264–241	First Punic War (war with city-state of Carthage)
241	Rome conquers all of Etruscan's lands
218–201	Second Punic War
149	Third Punic War begins
146	Third Punic War ends with Carthage destroyed.
55	Julius Caesar invades Britain
44	Caesar murdered
31	Cleopatra commits suicide and Egypt becomes part of the Empire

CE

43	Britain finally conquered by the Romans
60–61	Revolt in Britain led by Boudicca
64	Fire destroys much of Rome
79	Vesuvius erupts destroying Pompeii and Herculaneum
80	Colosseum built in Rome
122	Construction of Hadrian's wall across northern England begins
410	Romans leave Britain
455	The tribe known as the Vandals destroy Rome
476	The end of the Roman Empire

Glossary

aqueduct an arched bridge with water running in a canal on top to bring water to cities

architect a person who designs and draws plans for buildings

atrium a hole in the roof of a *domus* that lets in light

census an official count of the number of people who live in an area or country

daub see wattle and daub

domus a large Roman house

engineers people who design and construct buildings and roads

Etruscans people from Etruria, a region in northern Italy. Before the Romans, the Etruscans were the greatest civilization in Rome.

furnace a large oven used to produce heat for buildings or to melt or burn metals and waste

insulae Roman apartments. *Insulae* could be up to seven or eight stories high.

marble a type of stone often used in building

mosaics pictures made from small colored tiles pieced together and stuck into postion on floors.

ornate highly decorated

pergola an archway designed for plants to grow around in a garden

philosopher a person who studies human behavior and life

sewage human waste. The Romans built underground tunnels called sewers for the sewáge to flow through. The sewers emptied into the River Tiber.

shrine a place of religious worship. A shrine would often have a statue of a god inside it.

status symbol a precious object or possession that shows that the owner is wealthy, since only the rich can afford it

strongbox a heavy box that can be locked to keep valuables safe inside

viaduct an arched bridge with a road on top

wattle-and-daub walls walls made of sticks woven together and covered in mud or clay. The mud or clay dries to make the wall solid.

Index

Resources and Web Sites

Look Inside: A *Roman Villa* by Richard Dargie (Raintree, 2000)

Rich and Poor in Ancient Rome by Richard Dargie (Smart Apple Media, 2005)

Stories in Art: Mosaics by Nathaniel Harris (PowerKids Press, 2008)

Web Sites

Due to the changing nature of Internet links, PowerKids Press has developed an online list of Web sites related to the subject of this book. This site is updated regularly. Please use this link to access this list: http://www.powerkidslinks.com/acrl/homes/